# This Port Orchard Life

essays of small town life
by Carol DiMarco

Blue Forge Press
Port Orchard ✽ Washington

This Port Orchard Life
Copyright 2009, 2019
by Carol DiMarco

First eBook Edition April 2019
First Print Edition September 2009
Second Print Edition April 2019

ISBN 978-1-59092-926-1

All rights reserved, including the right to reproduce this book or portions thereof in any form whatsoever, except in the case of short excerpts for use in reviews of the book.

For information about film, reprint or other subsidiary rights, contact: blueforgegroup@gmail.com

This is a work of fiction. Names, characters, locations, and all other story elements are the product of the authors' imaginations and are used fictitiously. Any resemblance to actual persons, living or dead, or other elements in real life, is purely coincidental.

Blue Forge Press
7419 Ebbert Drive Southeast
Port Orchard, Washington 98367
360.550.2071 ph.txt

*to my family*

# Acknowledgements

My sincere thanks to the people who have encouraged, taught, inspired and supported me over the years:

Dr. Margaret Scarborough, Rodika Tollefson, my parents, siblings, partner, children, and grandchildren, and my good friends and neighbors in beautiful Port Orchard, Washington.

# Table of Contents

| | |
|---|---|
| Got Wood? | 11 |
| The ChickenKeeper | 15 |
| Won't You be My Neighbor | 19 |
| Treasure Hunt | 23 |
| Traveling in Circles | 27 |
| Supreme Bean | 31 |
| Straight as an Arrow | 35 |
| Spa Day | 39 |
| Signs of the Time | 43 |
| Searching for Spring | 47 |
| Rub-a-Dub-Dub, Twenty-four Chickens in a Tub! | 51 |
| Henny Penny: The New Red, White and Blue! | 55 |
| Pass It Forward | 59 |
| One of THOSE Days | 65 |
| An Ode to Cookie Dog | 69 |
| Big Yellow Bus: Time Machine into the Future | 73 |
| Go Fly a Kite | 77 |
| Goodbye Jule, God's Speed | 81 |
| Help Save a Port Orchard Life | 85 |
| Let It Rain | 89 |
| Liebchen Equals Little Love (Again!) | 91 |
| Ma Bell... HELP! | 95 |

# This Port Orchard Life

essays of small town life
by Carol DiMarco

# Got Wood?

My editor's challenge to me, is to engage men, not just women, with my stories. Talk about life in Port Orchard. Keep it to five hundred words or less. She might as well ask me to orchestrate world peace. (Just kidding, boss!)

I acknowledge she is correct. I do write from a female perspective, because, well, I am a female. But I'm no girly girl; more of a guy's gal really. I can wrangle my goats and chickens with ease. Build a barn. Handle a rifle. Drive an eighteen-wheeler.

I have decided to prove I can speak and write "man." I am dedicating this column to all the men in Port Orchard. I have chosen a very manly subject and title. The subject: Wood. The title: Got Wood?

Not just any wood, but the wood that is created when our delightful Port Orchard spring whips up wind gusts to 50 mph and trees come a tumblin' down. I have noticed wind blown trees in Port Orchard are peculiar. They rarely fall in an open field or a remote forest. They come down on Sedgwick, Mullenix, Mile Hill... any and all of our main roads. They always manage to bring power lines down with them and those power lines, no matter where they are, are always connected to my house.

My power never comes back on quickly enough for my liking. However, I must applaud the Public Works folks. Those windblown trees are cleared off the road, cut into eight-inch rounds, thrown in the back of their pickups and driven away in record time. The only evidence left of these fallen giants? A few wind blown leaves.

Not only do these hardworking public servants brave the storm and appear at a moment's notice, they drive their own vehicles! I imagine this saves the time of going into the Public Works Yard and picking up their official vehicles. So ardent are they in their pursuit of public safety, I have even witnessed several crews appearing at the same fallen tree and arguing about who should take it away.

Last week I had an opportunity to speak with a gentlemen who was just finishing up with a mammoth fallen big leaf maple; his full sized pickup filled four feet above the sideboards.

"Got wood?" I jested.

"Yup," says he, eyeing me somewhat warily.

"What does the city do with all that wood?" I continued.

"The city?" he replies.

"Oh, do you work for the county?"

"The county?" he asks. "Well, I need to be moving on, little gal. Got firewood to unload and stack up." He hopped in his truck and drove away. "Nice talking with you."

So, I may never know what government agency I should thank for clearing our roads after the storm. But I am joyful in the knowledge that those fallen giants are being put to good use, somewhere, by someone. Recycle. Reuse. It is a great Port Orchard life.

# The ChickenKeeper

I'm not a "joiner." Not because I don't honor being a part of a larger group. Kindred souls with like minds. Affirmation of my ideals. I just do not have time to attend meetings, events, whatever, that operate on a neat and tidy timeline in direct conflict with my usually chaotic schedule.

Even if I could be seduced into joining an organization, then there is the intimidating question of which group to choose. There are so many local and national entities that I emphasize with. Which one gets my precious time? The Kitsap Food Co-op? Juvenile Diabetes Association? Autism Society of Washington? AARP? Kitsap County Food Bank?

The list goes on and on. Sending money is easier but, I

don't have a lot of discretionary funds right now. Unless, of course, there are cookies involved. I am an avid supporter of any group of small children who will reward my generosity with boxes of cookies.

No, for practical reasons, I am not a joiner. Then why am I sitting on the tailgate of my farm truck at 8:30 AM, on a beautiful Saturday morning, waiting for the start of the Southworth Art and Garden Fair?

The Southworth Art and Garden Fair is an annual event hosted by the incredibly gracious Cynthia and Tony Mora of Rodstal Farm. Tony and Cynthia are very active in the local farm and natural foods community. Their energy is boundless.

Cynthia saw an ad I placed online for chicken tractors. It was an anonymous ad, so she didn't know it was me. She emailed me and asked if I would like to display one of my portable chicken coops at their fair. I wrote back, announcing it was me, and on a whim, agreed to participate in the fair.

I really like and respect Cynthia and Tony. Cynthia is always educating me about me about all the local farm groups. I figured it would be fun to finally get to participate in one of the many events Cynthia spoke about.

There was only one small problem. The only chicken tractors I had built were in my head. I dreamt about designs. I imagined joyful chickens traveling the fields in their mobile home. I'd wake up in the morning and write down all the different ideas and images.

Oh, they were beautiful. Well thought out. Functional, safe and aesthetically pleasing. They just didn't exist in the real world we all live in.

Well, I promised the Moras, so I better get started. I grabbed my notebook of dream ramblings. Pretty random. Maybe there's some plans online? No. Lots of questions from others. A couple of grainy photos and some really awful designs. So much for the world wide web.

Guess I'm on my own. I pulled my car out of the garage, which officially transforms my garage into my workshop. I spent a few minutes, ok, an hour, hunting down all my tools amongst the myriad of precious clutter. I dragged the cedar, sun wood and fencing out of my thirty-nine year old farm truck and went to work.

Thirty hours (over the course of five days) later my chicken tractor was complete. And, if I do say so myself, it was everything I dreamed. Fully functional, aesthically pleasing and a hit at the fair. It even housed amazingly life-like cardboard chickens my daughter, Jennifer, had created and strategically placed throughout the tractor.

I got to meet lots of chicken people and wanna-be chicken people. They loved my craftwomanship and were insatiable in their want for chicken raising knowledge. Friends and neighbors came by to coo and cackle about my lovely design. So my daydreams became a pleasant reality and the ChickenKeeper® mobile coop was born, in this, my Port Orchard life.

# Won't You Be My Neighbor

Turn on the TV news, read any big city paper, surf the web. Bad news is everywhere. Recession just around the corner. Jobs down. Homicides up. If it bleeds, it leads.

It is enough to break your heart and weaken your spirit. My parents speak of safer times, gentler times, simpler times. Honor, compassion, generosity and neighborhood were not just words but actions and real places.

Come with me, not back in time, but step in time, to the heartbeat of my community, Port Orchard. Witness with me that those elusive qualities and places of my parents' era still live.

Maria is a single mom, working two jobs with three small children. She always has a wave and a smile as she bustles by, dropping her kids at daycare, gardening in her small yard, rushing off to job one or two.

I will never know where she finds the time, money or energy, but once a month she bakes bread. To just call it bread, does not begin to describe the aroma that wafts through our neighborhood from her kitchen. To just call it bread, does not illustrate the comic relief of her three little ones tearing up and down the street covered in flour and bits of sticky, sweet dough.

The alluring smell is soon replaced by a still steaming loaf of zucchini, spice, raisin, pumpkin, whatever delight she has created this month, sitting wrapped in a simple white towel on my porch. And my neighbor's porch to the left. And my neighbor across the street. Everyone's porch (six!) in our cul de sac. The same note written every month: "Thank you for being my neighbor. – Maria"

Maria gives us all the most precious of gifts, her time. In the hustle and often break neck speed of her life, of all our lives, she makes the time to acknowledge and bless her neighbors.

I can tell you that this genre of kindness is contagious.

It was hard not to notice that Maria's yard was getting pretty wild. No wonder, between work and children, I felt yard maintenance was probably pretty low on her list of priorities.

So when I cut my lawn, I cut hers. One day, when I was struggling to get my almost antique mower running, Mike, another neighbor, walked over with his ever present black bag of tools and worked on my machine for well over an hour until it hummed like new.

A few weeks later, when Maria's bread appeared on all our doorsteps again, fresh strawberries accompanied it, from Catherine's garden.

On trash day, empty garbage cans disappear from the curb and magically appear back on their porches.

Wind blown trees and branches transform into neatly stacked firewood.

Fresh laid eggs join the strawberries and bread.

A nod, a wave, a smile.

Honor, compassion, generosity, the heartbeats of my neighborhood in this Port Orchard life.

# Treasure Hunt

The planets align. The gods smile. Nostradamus never predicted this: I have three hours of free time. No where to go. No one to see. Nothing to do. Well, that's not completely true. I ALWAYS have something to do, but I have nothing that can't wait three hours.

Three hours! What fun, wonderful, exciting adventure can I pursue? "I'll clean my garage," I thought to myself. Yes, I know it is pretty sad when your idea of a fun adventure is cleaning your garage. But, I am getting pretty tired of always searching through what seems like tons of "you-never-know-when-you'll-need-this" stuff.

The odd ceramic tile. A carpet remnant. A drill with no chuck. Jars and jars of screws, nails, fasteners of every size and shape imaginable. The tire jack to a car I sold four years ago. A fish tank (I haven't kept fish in fifteen years!). A half bag full of organic compost. You get the idea.

I climb into my coveralls. Grab a permanent marker and a handful of lawn and garden bags. I march into my garage/workshop/dumping ground. I even have a plan of attack. First, throw out anything and everything I've had for one year or more. The theory being, if I haven't used or needed it for a year, chances are I never will. Then, I will drag everything out of the miscellaneous cubbies, shelves and toolboxes. Purge. Organize. Label. Repack. I am psyched!

I grab a large, ragged unmarked cardboard box off a top shelf. I pull on the yellow tape that seals it closed. It crumbles in my hand. This is one OLD box. Reaching inside I find a hard object wrapped in layers of newspaper. The Seattle Times, 1982.

1982 was an eventful year. Grace Kelly, Princess of Monaco, died in a car crash. Soviet dictator Leonid Brezhnev died. Argentina attacked the British-held Falkland Islands. I turned thirty. My youngest daughter was five. My eldest, nine. I was a single mom struggling to make ends meet; juggling two jobs and two daughters.

I carefully remove the last layer of paper to discover a brontosaurus. Not just any dinosaur, but a handmade, paper mache bright green bronto with no legs and one eye. An art project lovingly made by my youngest, Angela, twenty-seven years ago. Gotta keep that. I set it aside for display inside the house. Note to self: Call Angela.

Next out of the box is a very heavy eighteen inch long something also wrapped in layers of newspaper. I carefully peel back the paper, pausing occasionally to read an interesting 1982 article. This next discovery is a ceramic statue of two green and gold lizards and dragons with their front arms around each other and dozens of babies riding on their back, and scurrying around their feet. Lifting it up I read the letters JENNIFER neatly etched on the bottom. Oh, yes, 1982, the year my eldest discovered dragons, magic and such. The endless imagination of a nine year old. Second note to self: Call Jennifer.

I gently place the dragons next to the one eyed brontosaurus and continue unpacking he box. Watercolor scenes of forests. Multiplication tables painstakingly written in neat columns. Mother' Day cards. Tiny I love you notes. Hardened clay figures. Necklaces of macaroni. Each revealed treasure more precious than the last.

Reaching for the last item my tummy grumbled, insisting it was time to eat. I glance at my watch to find not three but five hours has passed. My "free" time is expired. My garage is littered with crumbled newspapers. I have to find prominent display places for a multitude of treasures. The garage reorganization will have to wait for another day, in this, my Port Orchard life.

# Traveling in Circles

I consider myself to be fairly well educated, perhaps not in the conventional sense with years of school (and subsequent debt) and letters in front of or after my name. No, I am a student of the Renaissance 3-S school of life. Common sense, street sense and book sense.

My common sense comes from a long lineage of matriarchal Italian women, stories of arriving in the new country, the old country and being a working mother.

My street sense comes from growing up in New York City in the 60s, sneaking into Spanish Harlem whenever my mother's watchful eye blinked and having an insatiable lust for adventure.

My book sense comes from an acquired love of reading, spawned by the mandatory voluminous reading list of eight years of parochial education and the ever vigilant nuns poised with disciplinary rulers.

Lately, I've been traveling from my home in Port Orchard into West Seattle several times a week for one of my (three) jobs, realtor for Gates Realty. My youngest daughter (and business partner) lives in West Seattle and we are working together on several transactions there.

Leaving Port Orchard means taking the Southworth ferry. Taking the Southworth ferry means I have forty whole minutes of unscheduled, uninterrupted time, an absolute luxury for me.

I decided that my 3rd S (book sense) could use some freshening up. I made a list of classics I always meant to read, but somehow the rest of my life got in the way. First on my list was John Steinbeck's Grapes of Wrath.

Having been out of school for more than thirty years, I had a vague memory of the story line: Hard times in America. One family's story. Turns out it was a bit more complicated than my synopsis memory.

I finished this American classic in four ferry rides. I recommend it, especially if you're feeling that life in America is currently less than idyllic. You will travel alongside Steinbeck's Joad family through ignorance, prejudice, violence, poverty, hunger and homelessness, in the era of the Depression.

This tenant farming extended family migrate cross country from the Midwest dust bowl to the alleged promise land of California. In the face of overwhelming odds and hundreds of miles from their home, the Joads share their meager resources with other starving families they meet on the road and in the migrant camps.

The Joads remind us that neighborhood is not a place but a state of mind, a generosity of spirit and a caring heart. I can't help but think that the generous and perseverant Joad family would fit in quite well in our Port Orchard. Real people facing real challenges, doing the best they can with grace and dignity.

# Supreme Bean

9:00 AM: I'm parked at my favorite java joint, drinking my "short breve ristretto not too hot four sugar latte..." wondering how I was ever seduced into paying three dollars for basically a tepid cup of joe with cream and sugar.

I know the answer to this. It is not just the coffee. It is the company: the barista ladies. Quick with a smile. Listen to my woes. Interested in my stories. Three dollars for a cup of joe and ten gallons of therapy... worth every penny. This sweet jolt of liquid energy and their smiles are my daily reward for work already done.

5:00 AM: Walk the dog... miniature dachshund who will absolutely not pee in the rain... (which means in Port Orchard he basically pees four days a year). Feed the dog: home made ground lamb, basmati rice and carrots. He has food allergies, or so he would have me believe. Feed the cat. Fifty dollars a bag of my-cat-has-kidney-problems-according-to-the-vet-who-I'm-sure-has-stock-in-this-pet-food.

Wash last night dinner dishes, which I was absolutely going to do last night until I got sucked into the latest schmaltz from the Lifetime Channel. Take out the trash and the recycle.

Make sure all (eight) of the outside bird feeders are full of tasty treats for my itinerant backyard guests. Throw a handful of fish food in the pond, jump into my coveralls and head across the street. It's now 6:00 AM.

Across the street is three acres of salmonberry, salal, huckleberries, cedar, fir, maple, blackberries, fruit trees, herbs, vegetables, pasture and twelve Australorp hens, two twin caramel pygmy does, two twin bucklings and one agouti wether. In order: Busta, Blackie, and the girls, Lil Bit and Gigi, Coco and Cinnammon and Prince William AKA Billy. Yes, it's true I've only named two of the hens but I'm working on it.

The next two hours I spent cooing and coddling, mucking and watering, feeding and weeding until all barnyard creatures are, at least for the moment, clean, full and content.

I peel off my jumpsuit. Ease into my forty year old VW bug. Drive five miles west on Sedgwick to my favorite java joint for my "short breve ristretto not too hot four sugar latte." A tepid cup of joe with cream and sugar, my reward for work already done, before I go to work; another day in my Port Orchard life.

# Straight as an Arrow

Seems like I am always building something.

A barn for my partner's expectant pygmy does. These does are about to be featured on the Jerry Springer Show as mothers of immaculate conception OR the Agouti buck we rescued was not quite as immature as it's former human would have us believe.

A corral for my grandchildren's thirty bunny rabbits, who just two months ago were only two adorable alleged male bunnies. Are you reading this, Mr. Springer?

A hoop house to protect my cornfield from my chickens who love corn and evidently (who knew?) love tasty corn plants.

My project list goes on and on. I am always on the

lookout for deals at my local lumber and hardware store. Deals and innovative ideas for using alternative materials.

I patronize Bob-Chris-Dan-Jeff-John-Mike-Patrick-Paul-Ron-Shelley-Vince Lumber and Hardware aka Arrow Lumber and Hardware of Port Orchard. I imagine they call themselves Arrow because they are straight shooters, honest, helpful, quick with joke and great ideas.

Also, I imagine trying to paint Bob-Chris-Dan-Jeff-John-Mike-Patrick-Paul-Ron-Shelley-Vince Lumber and Hardware on their store front sign would be a little cost prohibitive and hard to remember.

Oh I admit, when the gigantic chain lumber store opened in Port Orchard, I checked it out. It is a really good thing I brought my miniature dachshund, Cookie, with me or I'd still be wandering around lost in there.

Cookie led me out safely but not before I got to hear:

...you're building a what? (Hoop house.)

...that item should be on aisle 3,007 which is about quarter mile from the front of the store, left at Appliances, right at Plumbing etc.

...and my favorite, what's a little gal like you doing building a barn? (I'm serious. That's a verbatim quote.)

It only took one visit to this mega retail outlet to

reaffirm that no one (or thing) can replace Bob-Chris-Dan-Jeff-John-Mike-Patrick-Paul-Ron-Shelley-Vince Lumber and Hardware.

They know my name. My budget. My crazy, never-ending projects. And, yes, they will meet or beat anyone else's price.

They are what makes living in a small town delightful. They are not just a store. They are my advisors and friends in my always busy—but constructive—Port Orchard life.

# Spa Day

I am trudging down Sedgwick Road. Pretty good pace. One foot in front of the other. Left, right, left, right, left....Wait a moment, don't get the wrong idea. I am no power-walker-jogger-water gulping-cardiac-health nut.

I believe that God gave most of us two feet. One for a brake and one for a gas pedal. I am in pretty good shape, for someone who is older than middle age, but younger than old. I am walking today because I have to—neither of my vehicles are running. I have no one to blame but myself.

I park my two vehicles next to each other on my driveway. A 1968 VW bug. Old enough to be a classic but not mint enough to be classy (kind of like its owner). Name: Midnight. A 1973 GMC Sierra 3/4 ton pickup. My farm truck. Ugly as a toad. Runs like a stallion. Name: Big Blueberry.

You cannot park two vehicles next to each other, day in and day out and not expect them to talk. Small talk turns to gossip. Gossip turns to conspiracy. Conspiracy turns to revolution.

Big Blueberry: "So, the old gal's been working me pretty hard. Hay, hog panel, organic grain, gravel, lumber. She just never lets up!"

Midnight: "What are you complaining about big boy? You're built for that abuse. I am a lady. Sleek and low to the ground. My rear end practically bounces out of its chassis just driving down that gravel road to the farm."

Big Blueberry: "Your rear end looks fine from where I'm parked."

Midnight: "Oh hush, you big brute!"

Big Blueberry: "Listen up, little gal, what'ya say we teach her a lesson?"

Midnight: "I'm listening."

Big Blueberry: "We can both pretend to break down. That way we will get us a day off at the garage. Maybe some new oil, even a chassis lube."

Midnight: "Hmmm, chassis lube, now you have my attention."

Big Blueberry: "Let's keep it simple. Tomorrow morning, I'll just refuse to start."

Midnight: "Oh, that's perfect. Anything could be wrong with you. Out of gas. Dead battery. Alternator gone bad. Voltage regulator shot. You'll get at least one day in the garage."

Big Blueberry: "That's what I'm thinking."

Midnight: "I think I'll leak a little gas. Fumes in the cab. Small puddle on the driveway. That should really freak her out given all the VW bugs she's burned up in her past!"

And so the revolution began. Both my babies in the garage, diagnosis: uncertain. I do feel bad. They're right. I work them both pretty hard and they rarely get a break. Well, they got one now.

I've arrived at my place now, Blueboots Farm. Thanks to your company, that quarter mile driveway just felt like a leisurely stroll. Hopefully, my chickens are feeling productive today. They lay a dozen organic eggs a day, at $3.75 per dozen.

The garage just called and Big Blueberry does need a voltage regulator and Midnight needs some fuel lines replaced. That's going to run about 612 eggs worth of money for their little spa day. With gas at four dollars plus a gallon, looks like I'll be walking to the farm for awhile. Hope you'll join me again in this, my Port Orchard life.

# Signs of the Time

Lately, I've been noticing a lot of signs. Nothing apocalyptic but nonetheless profound. There are, of course, all the leftover political signs. Fading and askew, along the side of the road. Inane messages. Catchy slogans. Like so much waning rhetoric and (soon to be) broken promises, they all blur together.

I cannot help but wonder if our want-to-be and newly elected public servants couldn't learn a lesson from our least fortunate and their signs. These are the signs held in hand at busy intersections and grocery store parking lots. WILL WORK 4 $. TRAVELING PLEASE HELP. NEED FOOD. $ 4 GAS.

Straight forward, self-serving yet brutally honest. No I M 4 U here. These folks need help from us and offer nothing in return, save perhaps our sense that even in these hard times, we could be worse off.

Seeing these signs and their disheveled owners always elicits mixed emotions for me.

There, but for the grace of God, go I.

I will never whine again about being broke.

Do I have any cash money with me?

Do I have any cash money with me I can spare?

Is this a scam?

Didn't I read somewhere that these folks actually make a decent living panhandling?

Shame on you, DiMarco! Pony up.

And I usually do, as do others. Pull my car over, search for change or a dollar or two and give it to the sign holder. Compassion wins over cynicism. Gratitude for my life (as hard as it sometimes seems) wins over disdain for these strangers.

Generosity, in times of plenty, is hollow.

Generosity, in difficult times, is the stuff humanity is made of.

When presented with the stark needs of others and asked to help, in this Port Orchard life, we do say, yes we can.

# Searching for Spring

According to the calendar it is now officially spring. Whoever invented this arbitrary date has evidently not looked out their window recently. Spring is not in the air. Snow is in the air... and hail... and wind... and rain!

I am searching for spring. Oh, it's true the crocuses are up, even a few tulips. I can see tiny buds on the fruit trees and my favas, peas and spinach are poking through the ground. However, I am still chipping ice off my animal's water pails. I took a major flying beaner off my deck, with the help of my over enthusiastic dachshund, on a leash, and a lovely patch of ice.

The winter seems to drag on forever. My block is quiet and lonely as neighbors hunker down in their warm homes, safe from the unpredictable cacophony that is spring weather on the Kitsap Peninsula. Lawns are unkempt and in need of mowing. Flower beds are invaded by weeds that (evidently) even grow in winter.

I am searching for spring. Today it arrived. The wind blew away the dark clouds and a brilliant shining orb appeared in the sky. Could it be the sun? I was skeptical. I waited for the warm yellow light to disperse. I stared at the outside thermometer anticipating the mercury's inevitable downward spiral.

Then suddenly, the surest sign of spring appeared. My neighbor's door opened. Hesitantly at first, as if testing the temperature of newly drawn bath, they stepped on to their covered porch. Then, a beam of light emanated from their hand. A flashlight, in daytime? No. It was the sun reflecting off a shiny, brand new hand trowel.

What's that sound? The revving of a small car engine? I glanced down the street in the direction of the noise. Another neighbor, starts up their reluctant lawn mower, after its six month rest. A glance up, a smile and a wave.

Doors opened. Mowers roared. The clang of garden tools as they are called up into service again. Laughter. Children flying on skateboards. The joyful bouncing of a basketball. Talk of weather, the promise of summer, the never ending yard upkeep. My neighborhood has awakened from its longer winter nap and it is finally spring in this, my Port Orchard life.

# Rub-a-Dub-Dub, Twenty-four Chickens in a Tub!

I have twenty-four chickens living in my bathtub. They should be living on my farm but my sister (who has evolved into a formidable chicken expert) informs me that it is still too cold for new chickens to be in an unheated coop.

I have tried arguing with her. "Joannie, the chickens will be fine. These two breeds are from the Midwest United States and Australia. They are used to much colder weather than what we get on the Kitsap Peninsula."

"No," she says, "it's too cold."

"But they're six weeks old now and bumping into each other. I am sure toe picking and other nasty cannibalistic behavior will soon follow."

"No," she says, "it's too cold."

"Please sister, I cannot stand another day sanitizing the entire bathroom due to chicken dust. The cat is going to get a traumatic brain injury from throwing herself against the bathroom door. The dog is going to bark himself mute. It's time for the babies to go join their adult sisters on the farm, in the coop."

"No," she says, "it's too cold. However, I have an idea."

Now you need to know that when my sister has "an idea" there is no dissuading her off that path. Even though she is my baby sister and a very diminutive gal, she has a way of looking at me, raising one eyebrow, and assuming an all-knowing composure. In Italian we call it "faccia contendere." The dispute face. There is no arguing or questioning the dispute face.

"You need to insulate the coop, just the new section you built for the babies. Insulate the coop. Put in two red heat lamps. Put a thermometer on the wall and see if you can maintain a minimum 70 degree temperature overnight. If you can, then the babies can move into the coop."

Okay. So I spent my only day off running to the hardware store, buying very expensive foil enclosed insulation (so the chickens don't peck on fiberglass); taking it to the coop and insulating the walls, door and roof line of the baby section of the coop. I set up two red bulb heat lamps and laid down at least 12 inch depth of white shavings. Shut the door and said a silent prayer that in the morning the thermometer would read 70.

I slept fitfully, frozen chickens and other grizzly images tossed and turned me throughout the night. 5:00 AM arrived too soon, but I leapt from bed anxious to dash to the farm and read the thermometer.

Stepping outside, the rooftops and lawns were white with a hard frost. The overnight temperatures had plummeted. Standing outside the coop door I paused, a silent prayer for warmer climes inside, on my lips. I opened the door and was greeted by a rush of warm air. The thermometer read 72 degrees. The chickens' new home was ready. My sister was right (again!) and suddenly it was spring in this, my Port Orchard life.

# Henny Penny: The New Red, White and Blue!

Oh, I know I'm going to regret this. I prefer to keep my stories light, anecdotal, intimate. A little peek at my always changing life and schedule. A slice of DiMarco pie.

But not today. Today I am on a soapbox, a mission. Today I am starting a campaign against one of our most revered symbols, the American bald eagle. Perhaps the word *against* is little strong. I am starting a movement *for* the American chicken. My farm is under siege by a devious, hungry symbol of the USA.

The first attack was thwarted by my ever vigilant neighbor, Lisa, (guardian to her own 50+ chickens). She made a lot of noise and scared the eagle off. He dropped the hen he held in his talons, but he had already eaten two others.

The dropped hen, I'm happy to say, recovered on a week long diet of hand fed salmonberries, organic layer crumble and lots of TLC. She has been renamed Phoenix for her ability to resurrect from her near death experience.

The second attack he was much bolder. He landed less than three feet from where my best friend Connie was weeding and tried to grab a heritage turkey. She tossed an empty five gallon water jug at him. He dropped the bird and flew off. The turkey was not injured.

This six foot wing span eagle has decided that my flock of hens is really an all day, all you can eat, free buffet. I am not happy about this. My flocks are free range. I am a city-born gal, learning farmer. I have not reconciled myself to the "acceptable loss theory" of farming and animal husbandry. I want it all. I want my girls to roam free. I don't want any predators to mess with them.

My twenty hens have names, personalities and always serve as my oasis, my zen time—plus, they give me eggs. This eagle, on the other hand, doesn't appear to serve any purpose. No eggs, no meat, no sweet cackle, coo or song.

So let's recap the positive points of each species:

American hen: eggs, meat, fertilizer, companionship, pest control and has been here since the birth of our nation.

American eagle: nothing, nothing, nothing and nothing.

I'm telling you now, if this big bully continues his murderous assaults, it's just a matter of time before our weapon of choice will change from an empty five gallon water jug to a— Well, nevermind.

So, join with me in writing your congress person. Join the campaign to make the American hen our national symbol and save me from fifty years in a Federal prison and a million dollar fine. Please help me continue to enjoy my Port Orchard life!

# Pay It Forward

Bad news seems to be the mantra of the day. Unemployment up. Savings are down. Record foreclosures. Dropping property values. Rising taxes. Hard working people are having trouble staying afloat, providing for their immediate family's basic needs.

Acts of kindness are easy in easy times. But no one I know is experiencing easy times. Some say, as times get harder, people will get harder. This has not been my experience. It is with great joy that I have witnessed or been told about the generosity, compassion and kindness of the folks in our community.

In line at one of our local discount grocery outlets, a young mother, with several small children, carefully unloads her cart on to the conveyor. I watch as she tallies the cost of each item in her head, a worried look on her face.

No frivolous purchases here. Nutritional foods. Milk. Diapers. Soap. The cashier hits the total button and the young mother's face tells us all it is obviously more than she can pay. $9.00 over her budget, her cash.

Before she can be embarrassed... before she has to make the tough decision of what she can live without... the gentlemen, behind her in line, quietly hands the cashier a ten dollar bill, smiles at the young woman and says, "my pleasure." She shyly mumbles a surprised thank you, gathers her children and groceries and leaves the store.

I gently touch the gallant elderly gentlemen on the elbow and say, "That was very kind, sir." He smiles and responds, "I know what it feels like to do without. I'm happy to help."

My very diminutive sister, Joannie, returns home from an out-of-town trip. She has to catch the ferry from Fauntleroy back to Port Orchard. She is waiting to walk on the boat with several pieces of luggage larger and heavier than she is.

She cannot fit through the turnstile with her bags so she waits patiently for the Washington State Ferry worker to open the door to the terminal for her. Unfortunately, the WSF worker loads all the vehicles before she allows my sister to board.

This leaves Joannie and her huge bags confronted with tightly packed vehicles on the car deck and no path to the elevator. As she tries to get the attention of a deckhand, a gentlemen in a Gaelic kilt approaches her and says, "Follow me."

He finds a path through the maize of cars and leads my sister up the car ramp to a stairway entrance. Joannie stares at the steep stairs and begins to protest. This Scottish prince of a man lifts up all her luggage and carries it effortlessly up the two flights of stairs to the passenger deck. "Have a nice evening," he says. The good Samaritan disappears into the crowd as quietly as he first appeared. My sister calls, "Thank you!" after him.

A dear friend of mine scoured her home with her two young sons for all their loose change. Sofas, pillows, under beds, jars, piggy banks, no hiding place was left unturned in their search for coins. They gathered their booty painstakingly counting it all up and dreaming and planning what special treats it would bring the boys.

Then they heard of a family whose dad had been ill and lost two weeks work. This family was struggling with an already tight budget and the missed work wages cut them deeply.

The treats would wait, even the children agreed. They cashed in their bounty and my friend gave it to the mom of the family in need. "Are you sure you can afford this?" she exclaimed, thankfully.

"We are okay right now and soon your family will be too. Pay it forward."

Last weekend I spent two hours in the urgent care

clinic for a mysterious eye ailment. They prescribed antibiotic drops and advised to see an eye doctor if I did not experience noticeable improvement in forty-eight hours. Two days later my eye is worse. I am sitting in the waiting room of my ophthalmologist's office. I am anxious. No, actually, I'm completely freaked out. I do not like doctor' offices. My vision is blurry. My eye really hurts. The only reason I'm not running screaming from the room is my sister is with me, calming me down with her mere presence.

My cell phone rings, my custom ringtone, chickens cackling. I am embarrassed because I usually mute my ringer in public places in the company of non-chicken fanatics. I quickly push the side button, silencing the ring.

A woman sitting across from me asks, "Do you write for the paper?"

"I do," I respond.

"Your ringtone gave you away. I loved your column about chickens becoming the new national bird."

"Thanks," I say.

A simple compliment from a kind stranger and I am suddenly feeling less afraid.

So today's column is one huge *thank you* to all of you out there whose kindness towards others enriches all our Port Orchard lives.

# One of THOSE Days

Last week, I experienced a day when nothing would go my way. My car wouldn't start. Granted, she's forty years old, and probably getting real tired of my daily eighty mile commute to job #3. But I count on her to transport me faithfully, without issue or complaint. After twenty minutes of coaxing, cajoling and finally, some not so gentle language, she cranked over.

I'm rattling down the road, thirty minutes late for my farm deliveries, when out of no where a pterodactyl landed in the middle of the road, twenty feet from my car. I hit my brake pedal hard, barely missing what turned out to be a magnificent blue heron that had evidently mistaken my '68 VW Bug for a tasty snack.

Heart racing at my close call, I pulled over on to the shoulder to gather my wits about me. After a few moments, I turned my head back to merge onto the road only to see twenty-nine dozen organic eggs, that were previously neatly stacked on my rear seat, broken and tossed all over the back of my car.

Banging my head on the steering wheel for a few moments (a technique I use to gather my thoughts), I head back to my farm to clean up my car, collect more eggs and take a few aspirin.

On the road again, new eggs on board, I finally arrive at my last delivery. I gather the last two dozen eggs and walk to my final customer's back door. Ambling down the long drive, I experience an eerie sensation of being watched. I pause, look around, nothing and no one. What's that? Out of the corner of my eye I see a bright flash of yellow fly from one cedar to another. Glancing in the direction of the flash, I see nothing in the trees.

I'm about to place the eggs on the porch when a winged griffin (ok, a huge yellow tabby, at least twenty lbs!) flies through the air and lands right on my last two dozen eggs. Five second slow motion frame: She waves her paw menacingly in my face... bounces off the egg cartons to the ground... the eggs are falling... falling...

I bolt upright in my bed. My radio alarm blinks 5:00 AM, blaring Daniel Powter's Bad Day. I rub my eyes and vow *never* to eat rocky road ice cream at midnight again, in this my Port Orchard life.

# An Ode to Cookie Dog

Our dog is dead. Cookie. Cookie Dog. Cookie Man. The Cookster. Big Dog. These are a few of the terms of endearment we called our dog. Our dog was a twelve pound (sometimes fourteen pound, depending on treat consumption) red miniature dachshund. He was eight years old. He was a gift to me and my life partner from our daughters. He was six weeks old when we brought him home. He fit in the palm of my hand.

Everyone we know in Port Orchard knew Cookie. The lumber yard, the java joint, the corner grocery store; all would ask: "How's guard dog? How's Cookie Monster? Why didn't you bring Cookie in today?"

Folks say we "humanize" our pets. Treat them like people, members of our family. But we could never turn Cookie into a human, because he was better than any human we have ever met.

He loved everyone, with no agenda or expectations. He was always joyful to see us, no matter our mood, our appearance, our net worth. He was a gift from God and our blessing to care for him.

He died suddenly, in the presence of his vet, Dr. Jeff. We are not sure what killed him. He had degenerative disc disease, but this should not have killed him. He had a heart murmur, but not a serious one. He had a slightly enlarged liver that was not life threatening. We did not request a necropsy.

What we do know, is he passed, without pain, in the company of a doctor who cared for him deeply. He died because it was his time.

We know that the silence in our home is deafening. No clicking of his little nails on the hardwood floors.

We know that our meals are no longer joyful, without the nudging of a little nose on our shins for morsels.

We know that the bed is colder without his burrowing presence and head on the pillow.

We know that the blanket on the couch will never again be warmed by his sleeping body.

We know that his brother, Mikey, is upset that he can't find Cookie anywhere in the house or yard.

We know the squirrels, moles and neighborhood horses are sighing with relief because Big Dog can no longer terrorize them.

We know that there will always be a hole in our hearts that no one will be able to fill.

We buried Cookie on our farm, alongside three chickens and a baby goat.

We know he is running through his celestial pasture, wagging his tail, terrorizing one and all, in his new Port Orchard afterlife.

# Big Yellow Bus: Time Machine into the Future

Early morning Friday, driving down Sedgwick Road, running around like a possessed person. Tying up loose ends. Working on my honey-do list. Trying to complete one million and one projects before I start my fourth (new) job on Monday.

Up ahead, a big yellow bus is stopping to pick up some children at their bus stop. I slow, turn on my flashers, out of respect for the safety of the children, (and to make sure someone in too much of a hurry doesn't land in my back seat!).

A young mother, watches as her child boards the bus. Her eyes tracing the child's every step. Up the stairs. Down the aisle. In the seat. Her gaze is pensive? Apprehensive? Focused? A younger child and a big red dog hover near the mom, bored, wanting to go back inside on this chilly November morning.

The big yellow bus lumbers down the road with its precious cargo safely in place. I pause to wonder what it feels like to be a young parent in such uncertain times. What kind of world will our children, grandchildren inherit?

How do we explain such tumultuous times to our progeny? Do we turn off the TV filled with combative political ads? Do we unsubscribe to the mainstream papers where everything that bleeds leads? Do we pretend that all is well with the world? How do we caution our children, keep them safe, without terrorizing them?

The big yellow bus slows again. I fantasize it is speaking to me, to all of us. Slow down. Stop (the madness). Caution. Think of the well-being of the children. The children who deserve a safe world. The children who deserve a prosperous economy.

The big yellow bus starts up again. No more stops now. It delivers our young citizens to the safety and education of our public schools. School, where they will learn about our past, present and future as a people. Let the children learn well. The children who are the future for all of us, in this Port Orchard life.

# Go Fly a Kite

I am having a little trouble writing this column. Normally, I meditate a few moments on my (often) frantic schedule and a clever little anecdote just flows from my pen to paper.

Not so today. The problem? I'm relaxed. I just returned from three no pressure-no phone calls-no deadlines-no customers-no farm crisis days on the Long Beach Peninsula: my mini vacation at the International Kite Festival.

I packed up one sister, Joannie, one cousin, Beth, one friend, Connie and two dogs (Cookie and Mikey) and headed southwest out of Port Orchard for the three-plus hour drive to Long Beach, Washington. The weather was wild, strong winds and torrential rain. The coast was breathtaking. The Pacific Ocean, surly and brown with foam.

We arrived at our destination, a rustic, tiny cabin on Shakti Cove, Ocean Park, just a few miles outside of Long Beach. We unloaded our cars, stiff and sore from the long ride, but ready for our beach adventure.

Wednesday became Thursday, Thursday became Friday and, in what seemed like the blink of an eye, it was time to journey back home. In that blink of time we:

> ate too much
> slept too long
> ran the pups on the beach
> photographed the amazing array of kites
> ate too much again
> bought googahs we didn't need
> watched bad movies on a VCR (!)
> ate too much another time
> flew our own kites
> and talked and talked and laughed and laughed (like only four women can).

The ride back was filled with the genre of silence that is born of light hearts, full tummies and great company.

We arrived home just before sunset and I could not resist "just checking on my girls", the chickens at the farm. Our vacation was wondrous but I am ready to jump back into my often too busy but always fulfilling Port Orchard life.

PS: Need to relax? Go fly a kite. I highly recommend it!

# Goodbye Jule, God's Speed

My Aunt Julia died this week, in her sleep. She was ninety-five years old. She was the eldest of my mother's three sisters. She was my sister Joannie's godmother. We called her Aunt Jule.

Aunt Jule was unusual for our Italian-American family. She was quiet. She was tall. I am not really sure how she survived ninety-five years in our clan with her reserved demeanor.

We are not a shy or quiet people. Or as my mother, Eleanor, would say to guests whenever we were alarmingly loud or gesturing too dramatically: "We are an *alive* people."

I remember watching my Aunt Jule at our weekend extended family dinners aka "The Club." While all around her were screaming, gesturing and generally behaving Italian, Aunt Jule would calmly observe the fray.

It became my childhood quest to get a rise out of Aunt Jule. I was only successful once, and that was by accident. My cousin Wayne and I were digging up a raised garden space behind the duplex home Aunt Jule shared with her husband, Jack, daughter, Dawn, son, Gerald and mother-in-law, Gerlanda.

While turning the soil we hit what appeared to be solid concrete. Many hours later we discovered our "raised garden" was in reality an ancient fish pond. Aunt Jule came out to inspect our progress. Upon seeing the unearthed pond, she exclaimed: "Imagine that, fish in the garden!" And then she laughed.

This may not seem such a demonstrative exclamation, to those of you outside my immediate family. But given Aunt Jule's usual low key pose, this was the equivalent of her jumping up and down and doing the Tarantella.

It was startling for me to see Aunt Jule laugh. Almost fifty years after this fish pond archeological dig, it occurs to me Aunt Jule did not often laugh. There was a somberness about her that even my crazy family couldn't break through.

I do not know what secrets weighed on my Aunt Jule's spirit. I do know I will miss her. When I gaze at my backyard fish pond, I will remember Jule and hope she is laughing and dancing the Tarantella on the clouds above my Port Orchard life.

# Help Save a Port Orchard Life

Today I was going to talk about one of my jobs, Real Estate Professional for Gates Realty in Port Orchard. I was going to regale you with stories of always going the extra mile for my customers.

I would mention my daughter, Angela DiMarco and my sister, Joannie DiMarco, all part of the DiMarco Real Estate Team. Stories of our many challenging real estate adventures, the never ending support of our broker, would all combine to dispel forever the street myth that "realtors do nothing for their money."

Trinette was flattered that I would write about our work but she asked that I write about someone else. His name is Brock Haarstad. He is the five year old grandson of Leslie Enyeart, one of our Gates agents. As you are reading this, he is battling against leukemia. Brock is a bright, courageous little guy who has been fighting this disease for over a year.

Much like the action figures he so loves, he awakens every day to fight another battle. His first round of treatments, including a bone marrow transplant from his brother, Ryan, granted him a temporary remission. His cancer returned with a vengeance. He went through a second, brutal round of chemo although his doctors held out little hope for his survival. Brock had other plans. He made it through the chemo and received his second bone marrow transplant December 19.

Brock is now heavily sedated and in isolation while we all wait and pray that his body will respond favorably to the second transplant. He slept through Christmas. His hospital bed surrounded by unopened presents.

Leukemia is a cancer of the white blood cells, the cells in the body that normally fight infections. Most cases occur in children ages 3 – 7 years. In acute leukemia, cancerous cells multiply quickly and replace normal cells. Cancerous cells take over normal parts of bone marrow, causing bone marrow failure. Treatment options include chemotherapy, radiation therapy and bone marrow transplants; all of which Brock has been through.

No one should have to battle such an assault on the human body. No one, especially not a child.

Pray. Give blood. Give bone marrow.

Give Brock back his Port Orchard life.

# Let It Rain

I woke up his morning anxious to see if it was raining. I'm not sure why this happened. I do not believe it was an overnight or instantaneous change. This change in my life was gradual, subtle. I want rain. Need rain.

Everywhere I go people grumble about the rain...too much rain. Don't you hate all this gloomy weather? Strangers ask in passing conversation. I avert my eyes and mumble, very quietly, no, I want it to rain.

My rain barrels, the ones that water my animals, are empty. My newly seeded pasture needs rain. I have become, in spite of my cosmopolitan roots, a farmer. I stare in the mirror. How did this happen?

Me, a farmer? I grew up in New York City. No farmers in New York City. Farmers were the stuff of baby books. Old McDonald and the like.

I was a child of the 60s. Fearless. Reckless. Ran the rough streets. Staying out all night. Sleeping half the day away. Gave my parents every gray hair they have. Smoked. Drank. Generally behaved very badly. I was rough, tough and hard to handle.

In control of my universe, or so I thought.

Now I awaken at five AM searching the sky for nimbus clouds. I check my outside thermometer to see if hard frost is imminent. I fill five-gallon containers with warm tap water and lug them the quarter mile to my "off the grid" farm because the rain barrels are empty. No control of my universe here.

I say a silent prayer for rain.

In my youth, I believed I was indestructible. I didn't need faith. I had bravado. I didn't ask God for anything. I could buy, borrow or steal what I required. I believed I was fearless, courageous.

Fifty years later, I have discovered that all I really was—more than?—was a little crazy. It doesn't take guts to run the streets, just reckless abandon. It takes guts to be a farmer. Guts, faith, patience, hard work and hope.

I awaken now every morning hopeful for rain. Thankful for 35 instead of 29 degrees Fahrenheit. Greeted wildly by my flock of crazy chickens. Nuzzled gently (and sometimes not so gently!) by my small herd of goats. Watering, mucking, and checking the fields for a small miracle. One blade of timothy. Standing still and listening to the silence of frogs, wrens, robins and the neighbor's rooster.

Letting go and letting God be my partner in this my Port Orchard life.

# Liebchen Equals Little Love (Again!)

Bittersweet... Chocolate? Life? Love? No. None of those. Joey. Joey Liebchen, the newest member of our family. A 6 lb 3 oz bundle of energy, mischief, never-ending need and love. Yes, the rumors are true. I have a new dachshund.

Those of you who read my column regularly (thanks, Mom and Dad!) know that I recently lost my beloved dachshund, Cookie. I thought I could never love another dog. I resisted the very idea of anyone replacing Cookie.

Then one day I was cruising online and happened upon an ad for a ten week old dachshund. (Okay, so maybe I did type "dachshund" into the Google search engine.)

There was the yet–to–be–named Joey Liebchen...

posing with a football, biting a flower. I was falling fast.

Bitter. There is a way this dog looks at me. Wistful, with his head tilted to one side, daring me not to fall in love again. When he does this, he reminds me so much of Cookie, I get a literal pain in my heart.

Sweet. He will roll on his back for no apparent reason and demand I rub his belly.

Sweet. He will fall asleep, any time of day or night, the moment he gets on my lap.

Sweet. He believes pine cones are alive. Pounces on them every chance he gets.

Sweet. He burrows under the covers of my bed and nips at my toes.

Sweet. He lays across the back of my neck whenever we get in my car.

And get in my car we did. We visited everyone who knew and loved Cookie. The java joint, the lumber yard, the office, the grocery store, my farm customers, neighbors, co-workers, family and friends... all around Port Orchard, Joey was winning—and breaking—hearts.

Our last stop was my farm, where my goats and chickens live and Cookie is buried. Joey and I visited at his gravesite. Carrying Joey in my arms I set him down by the grave. He walked right up to the headstone, paused and made a sound I can only describe as a cat's purr; the sound Cookie would make when he was very content.

Joey then turned and gave me his best wistful, with his head tilted to one side, daring me not to fall in love again look. I knew that Cookie had blessed the latest chapter and newest member of this my Port Orchard life.

# Ma Bell... HELP!

3G, 4G, Apps, Bluetooth, Blueberry, Blackberry, Bump, Twitter and Flash. Fruit? CIA code names? Famous pirates? No. These are a few new words of a secret unintelligible language, obviously not meant to be deciphered by my people, the fifty+ year old tribe.

This covert dialogue is every where. Magazines, television, billboards, internet. It is spoken by sultry movie stars, nerds in glasses, roving gangs of geeks in vans, piñata-breaking dads... but not by me.

These spokespeople are always holding some sort of hybrid electronic device. It is hard to describe. It appears to be what would evolve if a TV remote, a pager, a phone, a teeny tiny computer, a toaster and a microwave were to combine and produce offspring.

My sister, Joannie, and I are enjoying some late night

TV show when one of the more convoluted ads for these devices air. A disembodied voice, joined by two disembodied hands holding the object, launches into a rapid fire description of all the functions of the mystery machine.

Bump... exchange contacts
Grind... coffee
Download... music
Shoot... photos
Scramble... eggs
Navigate... Paris
Play... scrabble
Decipher... foreign bus routes
Take over... the world!

Joannie and I turn slowly and gaze at each other, our eyes glazed over from this information assault.

I shrug my shoulders.

She does the same.

"What is it?!" I ask.

"A phone?" Joannie responds uncertainly.

"A phone?" I respond.

"Maybe," replies Joannie.

I glance at my battered, bruised, chunky, eight year old cell phone on the couch arm. Keys for the numbers 0 through 9. A dial button. A hang up button. That's all there is to it.

I show it to Joannie.

"*This* is a phone," I say, at least it is in my Port Orchard life.

www.ingramcontent.com/pod-product-compliance
Lightning Source LLC
Chambersburg PA
CBHW050043080526
44586CB00014B/1426